JOHN RUTTER

THE GIFT OF LIFE

SIX CANTICLES OF CREATION

FOR MIXED CHOIR (DOUBLE CHOIR IN MOVEMENT 3)
WITH ORCHESTRA OR CHAMBER ENSEMBLE

MUSIC DEPARTMENT

OXFORD
UNIVERSITY PRESS

OXFORD
UNIVERSITY PRESS

Great Clarendon Street, Oxford OX2 6DP,
United Kingdom

Oxford University Press is a department of the University of Oxford.
It furthers the University's objective of excellence in research, scholarship,
and education by publishing worldwide. Oxford is a registered trade mark of
Oxford University Press in the UK and in certain other countries

© 2015 Collegium Music Publications
Hymn to the Creator of Light © Oxford University Press 1993

Exclusively licensed Worldwide to Oxford University Press

John Rutter has asserted his right under the Copyright, Designs
and Patents Act, 1988, to be identified as the Composer of this Work

First published 2015

ISBN 978–0–19–341150–0

Printed in Great Britain on acid-free paper

CONTENTS

The first performance of *The Gift of Life* was given on 19 April 2015 at Preston Hollow Presbyterian Church, Dallas, Texas, by the Sanctuary Choir and Orchestra (director, Terry Price), conducted by the composer.

It has been recorded by the Cambridge Singers and the Royal Philharmonic Orchestra, conducted by the composer. The recording is on the Collegium label (COLCD 138).

Hymn to the Creator of Light was originally written in 1992 as an unaccompanied motet for the Gloucester Three Choirs Festival, in memory of Herbert Howells.

For texts, see p. 82. A programme note is available on the Collegium website: www.collegium.co.uk

Duration: 42 minutes

INSTRUMENTATION

The Gift of Life is available in two different instrumentations:

1. for full orchestra:

> 2 flutes
> 2 oboes
> 2 clarinets
> 2 bassoons
> 4 horns in F
> 3 trumpets in B flat
> 3 trombones (2 tenor, 1 bass)
> tuba
> 3 or 4 pedal timpani (1 player)
> percussion*
> harp
> strings (suggested minimum 4 - 4 - 2 - 2 - 2)

*2 players: glockenspiel, crotales, tubular bells, clash cymbals, suspended cymbal, snare drum, tambourine

2. for chamber ensemble

For details of this reduced orchestration, see the Oxford University Press website.

All performing material for both versions is available on hire
from Oxford University Press. Please specify, when ordering,
which version is required.

in honour of Terry Price
and in memory of Alice Marie Lind
commissioned by David and Miranda Lind

THE GIFT OF LIFE
Six Canticles of Creation

JOHN RUTTER

1. O all ye works of the Lord

Benedicite (from the 1662 BCP)
and Doxology (traditional)

Printed in Great Britain

OXFORD UNIVERSITY PRESS MUSIC DEPARTMENT, GREAT CLARENDON STREET, OXFORD OX2 6DP

4

*The sopranos and altos are intended to divide into three parts of equal strength, and if preferred, the first alto part may be sung by second sopranos, with all altos singing the second alto part.

S. bless ye the Lord: praise him, and ma - gni-fy him for ev - er.

A. bless ye the Lord: praise him, and ma - gni-fy him for ev - er.

T. bless ye the Lord: praise him, and ma - gni-fy him for ev - er.

B. O ye winds of God,

S. O ye fire and heat,

A. praise him, and ma - gni-fy him for ev - er.

T. praise him, and ma - gni-fy him for ev - er. O ye fire and heat,

B. bless ye the Lord: praise him, and ma - gni-fy him for ev - er.

(con Ped.)

2. The tree of life

Words: from the Collection of
Joshua Smith, New Hampshire (1784)

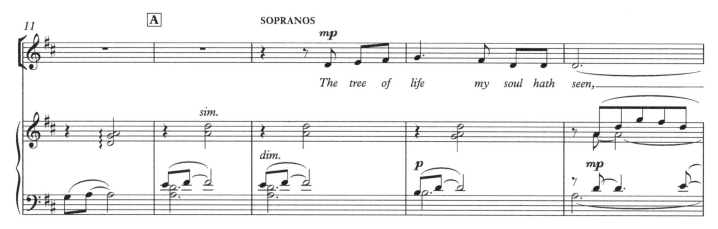

3. Hymn to the Creator of Light

Lancelot Andrewes (1555–1626), tr. Alexander Whyte
and J. Franck (1618–77), tr. Catherine Winkworth

Bar numbers in this movement start at 0 not 1, in order to match the numbering of the original unaccompanied version.

* Melody 'Schmücke dich' by J. Crüger (1598–1662)

4. O Lord, how manifold are thy works

Words from Psalm 104*

*The text from bar 118 onwards is by the composer.

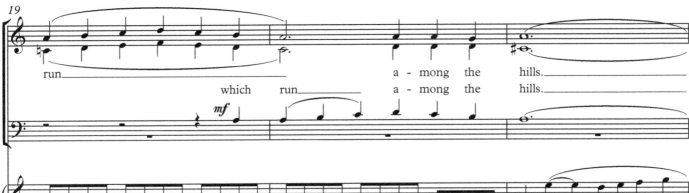

He send-eth the springs in - to the ri - vers:___ which

run____ a - mong the hills.____
which run____ a - mong the hills.____

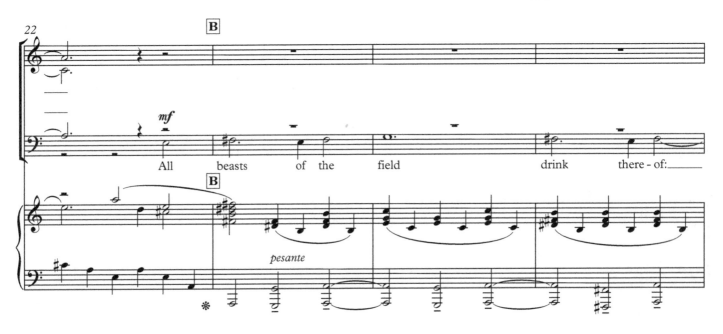

All beasts of the field drink there - of:____

*In these five bars, adjust the division of voices if necessary to achieve an equal balance.

and the fir-trees are a dwell-ing for the stork._____ The

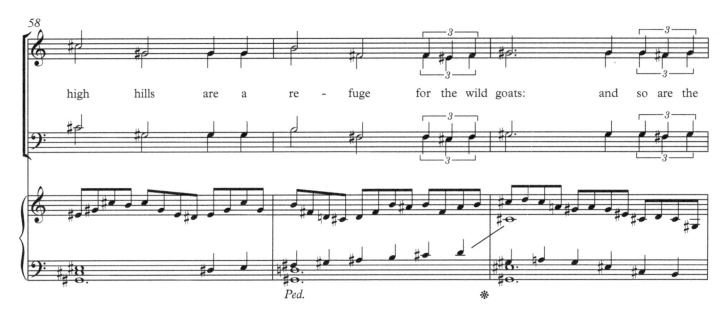

high hills are a re - fuge for the wild goats: and so are the

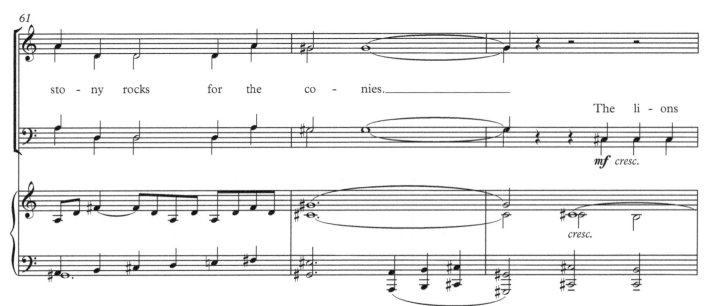

sto - ny rocks for the co - nies._____ The li - ons

work,_____ and to his la - bour un - til the eve - ning,_____ un - til the

(Choir unaccompanied)

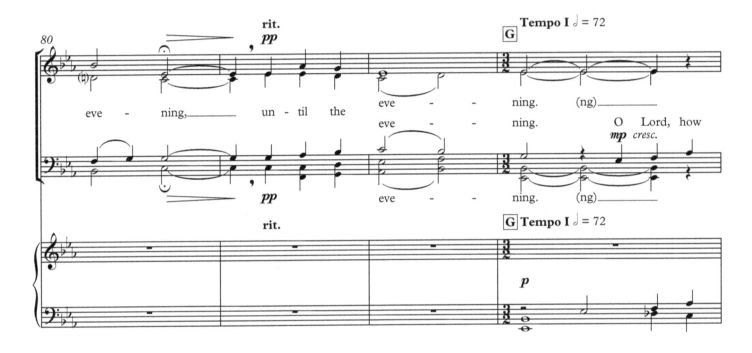

eve - ning,_____ un - til the eve - - ning. (ng)_____

eve - - ning. O Lord, how

eve - - ning. (ng)_____

how man - i - fold are thy works,_____ are thy_____

man - i - fold are thy works:_____ in wis - dom hast thou made them

works: the earth is full____ of thy rich - es,

all;   full of thy

rit.   Ⓗ a tempo

is full_____ of thy rich - es.____

rich - es,

rit.   Ⓗ a tempo

poco a poco cresc.   mf cresc.   f

The glo - rious Ma - jes - ty of the Lord shall en - dure for

ev - er:_____ the Lord shall re - joice in his works._____

up at his com - mand; To God on high be end-less glo - ry, praise and

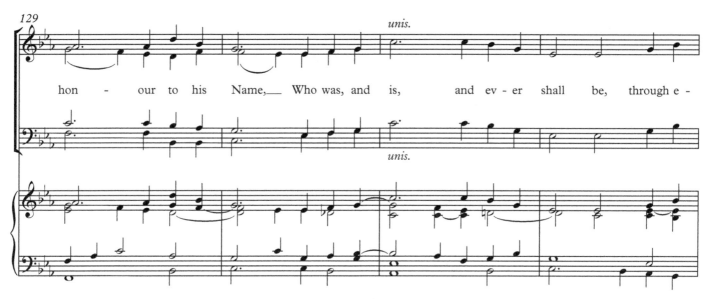

hon - our to his Name, Who was, and is, and ev - er shall be, through e -

-ter-ni - ty the same.

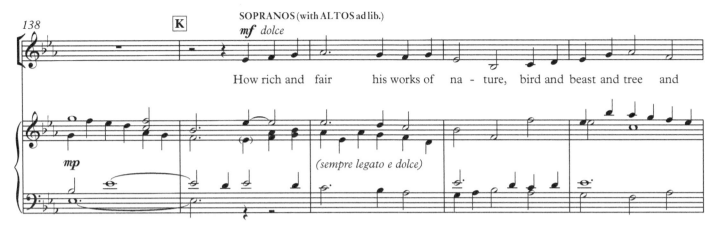

SOPRANOS (with ALTOS ad lib.)

How rich and fair his works of na - ture, bird and beast and tree and

flow'r; All that lives, and has its be - ing un - der God's al - migh - ty

pow'r! To him who reigns___ in end-less glo - ry,___ praise and ho - nour to his

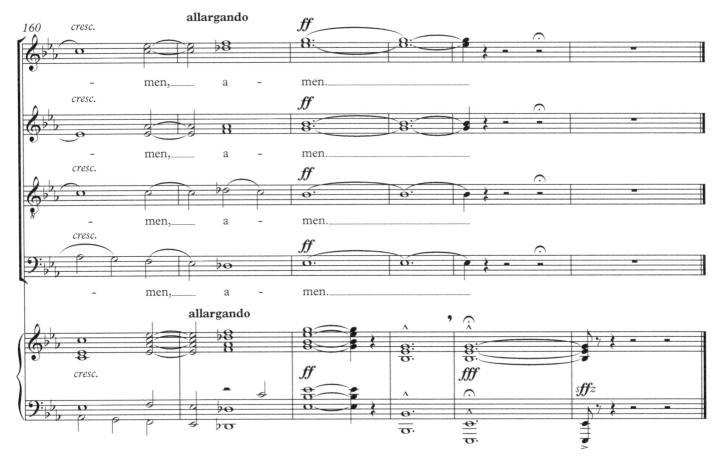

5. The gift of each day

Words by John Rutter

* If bars 3–7 are too low for the tenors, they can be sung by basses alone.

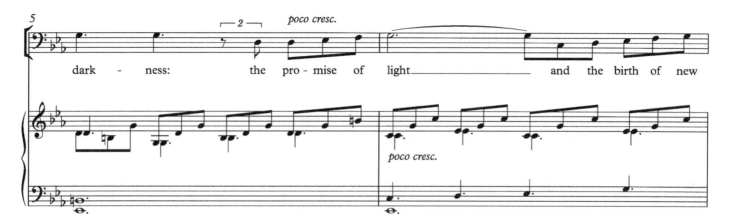

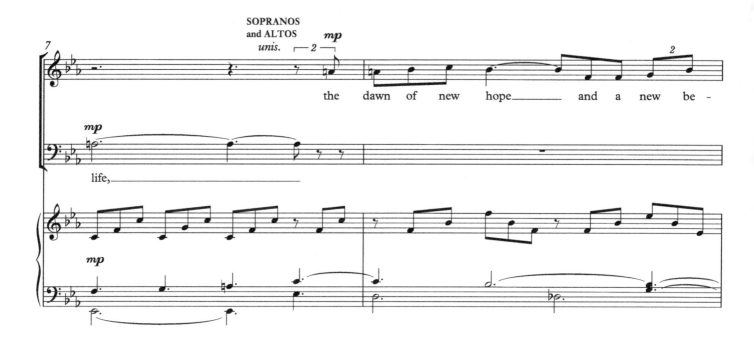

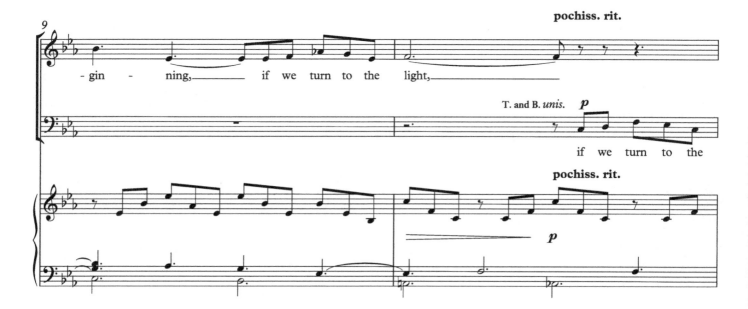

The gift of each day_____ stir-ring all a-

light;

-round us: the sights of the earth,_____ and sea,_____ and

sky,_____ For - ev - er fresh_____ as the day we first

mp
saw them, for - ev - er new as cre - a - tion's first
mp
mp
day.
accel.
B Poco più mosso ♩ = c.76
mf cantabile
Do - mi - ne, gra - ti - as a - gi - mus ti - bi; Lord God, we
mf cantabile
mf
give you thanks, bless - ing, and praise.
SOPRANOS mf più dolce
Be - hold cre - a - tion, so filled with

6. FINALE: Believe in life

Words by John Rutter*

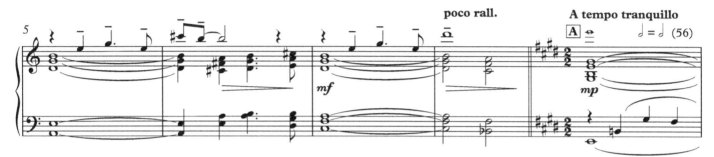

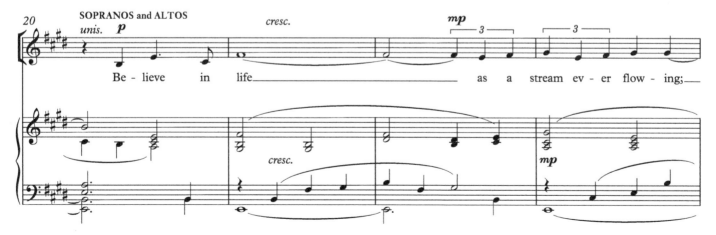

SOPRANOS and ALTOS
unis.

Be - lieve in life as a stream ev - er flow - ing;

* The text in bars 107–119 is from the Collection of Joshua Smith, New Hampshire (1784)

74

be - lieve in your dreams.

hopes,

The stream rolls

on - ward; all things must pass. Our earth - ly

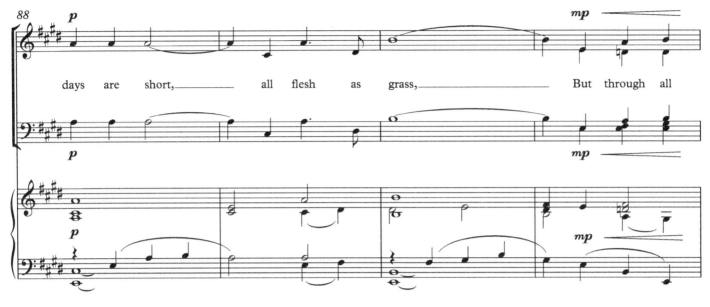

days are short,_____ all flesh as grass,_____ But through all

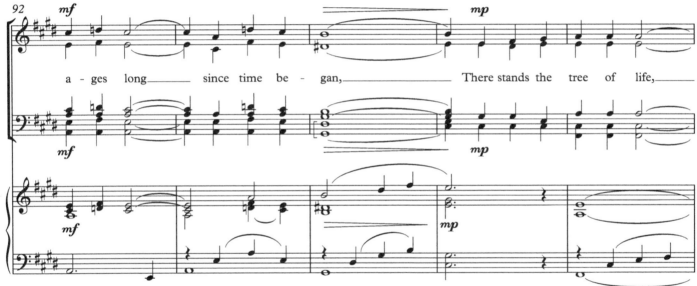

a - ges long_____ since time be - gan,_____ There stands the tree of life,_____

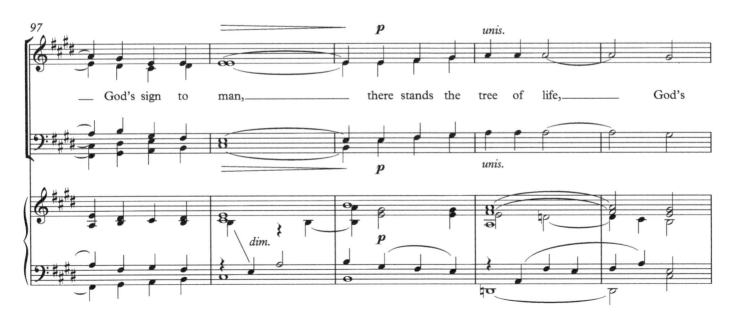

____ God's sign to man,_____ there stands the tree of life,_____ God's

* If sung solo, placed distant from main chorus if possible. If the passage is sung by chorus tenors, they should omit the first chorus tenor note in bar 119.

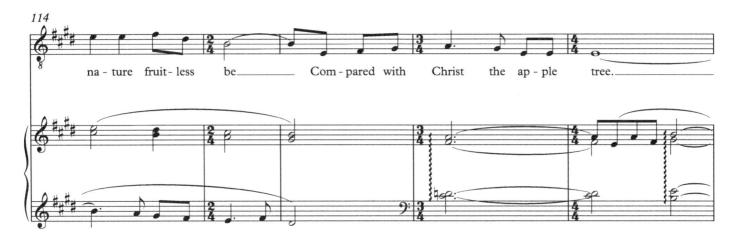

TEXTS

1. O all ye works of the Lord

O all ye works of the Lord, bless ye the Lord: praise him, and magnify him for ever.

O ye angels of the Lord, bless ye the Lord: praise him, and magnify him for ever.

O ye heavens, bless ye the Lord: praise him, and magnify him for ever.

O ye waters that be above the firmament, bless ye the Lord: praise him, and magnify him for ever.

O all ye powers of the Lord, bless ye the Lord: praise him, and magnify him for ever.

O ye sun and moon, bless ye the Lord: praise him, and magnify him for ever.

O ye stars of heaven, bless ye the Lord: praise him, and magnify him for ever.

O ye showers and dew, bless ye the Lord: praise him, and magnify him for ever.

O ye winds of God, bless ye the Lord: praise him, and magnify him for ever.

O ye fire and heat, bless ye the Lord: praise him, and magnify him for ever.

O ye winter and summer, bless ye the Lord: praise him, and magnify him for ever.

O ye dews and frosts, bless ye the Lord: praise him, and magnify him for ever.

O ye frost and cold, bless ye the Lord: praise him, and magnify him for ever.

O ye ice and snow, bless ye the Lord: praise him, and magnify him for ever.

O ye nights and days, bless ye the Lord: praise him, and magnify him for ever.

O ye light and darkness, ye lightnings and clouds: praise him, and magnify him for ever.

O let the earth bless the Lord: yea, let it praise him, and magnify him for ever.

O ye mountains and hills, bless ye the Lord: praise him, and magnify him for ever.

O all ye green things upon the earth, bless ye the Lord: praise him, and magnify him for ever.

O ye wells, bless ye the Lord: praise him, and magnify him for ever.

O ye seas and floods, bless ye the Lord: praise him, and magnify him for ever.

O ye whales, and all that move in the waters, bless ye the Lord: praise him, and magnify him for ever.

O all ye fowls of the air, bless ye the Lord: praise him, and magnify him for ever.

O all ye beasts and cattle, bless ye the Lord: praise him, and magnify him for ever.

O ye children of men, bless ye the Lord: praise him, and magnify him for ever.

O let Israel bless the Lord: praise him, and magnify him for ever.

O ye priests of the Lord, bless ye the Lord: praise him, and magnify him for ever.

O ye servants of the Lord, bless ye the Lord: praise him, and magnify him for ever.

O ye spirits and souls of the righteous, ye holy and humble men of heart, bless ye the Lord: praise him, and magnify him for ever.

O Ananias, Azarias, and Misael, bless ye the Lord: praise him, and magnify him for ever.

Glory be to the Father, and to the Son, and to the Holy Ghost;

As it was in the beginning, is now, and ever shall be: world without end. Amen.

*(Canticle of the Three Holy Children,
from the 1662 Book of Common Prayer)*

Praise God, from whom all blessings flow,
(Gloria in excelsis Deo)
Praise him, all creatures here below,
Praise him above, ye heavenly host,
Praise Father, Son, and Holy Ghost. Amen.

(Traditional doxology)

2. The tree of life

The tree of life my soul hath seen,
Laden with fruit, and always green;
The trees of nature fruitless be
Compared with Christ the apple tree.

This beauty doth all things excel;
By faith I know, but ne'er can tell
The glory which I now can see
In Jesus Christ the apple tree.
   The tree of life . . .

For happiness I long have sought,
And pleasure dearly I have bought;
I missed for all, but now I see
'Tis found in Christ the apple tree.

I'm wearied with my former toil,
Here I shall sit and rest awhile;
Under the shadow I will be
Of Jesus Christ the apple tree.
   The tree of life . . .

This fruit doth make my soul to thrive,
It keeps my dying faith alive;
Which makes my soul in haste to be
With Jesus Christ the apple tree.
   The tree of life . . .

*(from the collection of Joshua Smith,
New Hampshire, 1784)*

3. Hymn to the Creator of Light

Glory be to thee, O Lord, glory be to thee,
Creator of the visible light, the sun's ray, the flame of fire.
Creator also of the light invisible and intellectual,
That which is known of God, the light invisible.
Glory be to thee, O Lord, glory be to thee,
Creator of the light,
for writings of the law, glory be to thee,
for oracles of prophets, glory be to thee,

for melody of psalms, glory be to thee,
for wisdom of proverbs, glory be to thee,
experience of histories, glory be to thee,
a light which never sets.
God is the Lord, who hath showed us light.
(Lancelot Andrewes (1555–1626), tr. Alexander Whyte)

Light, who dost my soul enlighten;
Sun, who all my life dost brighten;
Joy, the sweetest man e'er knoweth;
Fount, whence all my being floweth.
From thy banquet let me measure,
Lord, how vast and deep its treasure;
Through the gifts thou here dost give us,
As thy guest in heaven receive us.
(J. Franck (1618–77), tr. Catherine Winkworth (adapted))

4. O Lord, how manifold are thy works
O Lord, how manifold are thy works: in wisdom hast thou made them all; the earth is full of thy riches.
Thou cover'dst it with the deep like as with a garment: the waters stand in the hills.
He sendeth the springs into the rivers: which run among the hills.
All beasts of the field drink thereof: and the wild asses quench their thirst.
Beside them shall the fowls of the air have their habitation: and sing among the branches.
He bringeth forth grass for the cattle: and green herb for the service of men.
The trees of the Lord also are full of sap: even the cedars of Libanus which he hath planted;
Wherein the birds make their nests: and the fir-trees are a dwelling for the stork.
The high hills are a refuge for the wild goats: and so are the stony rocks for the conies.
The lions roaring after their prey: do seek their meat from God.
The sun ariseth, and they get them away together: and lay them down in their dens.
Man goeth forth to his work, and to his labour until the evening.
O Lord, how manifold are thy works: in wisdom hast thou made them all; the earth is full of thy riches.
The glorious Majesty of the Lord shall endure for ever: the Lord shall rejoice in his works.
(from Psalm 104)

For all the gifts of God's creation fashioned by his mighty hand:
Earth and heaven, and all things living springing up at his command;
To God on high be endless glory, praise and honour to his Name,
Who was, and is, and ever shall be, through eternity the same.

How rich and fair his works of nature, bird and beast and tree and flower;

All that lives, and has its being under God's almighty power!
To him who reigns in endless glory, praise and honour to his Name,
Who was, and is, and ever shall be, through eternity the same. Amen.
(John Rutter)

5. The gift of each day
The gift of each day rising out of darkness:
the promise of light and the birth of new life,
the dawn of new hope and a new beginning,
if we turn to the light;

The gift of each day stirring all around us:
the sights of the earth, and sea, and sky,
Forever fresh as the day we first saw them,
forever new as creation's first day.

Domine, gratias agimus tibi;
Lord God, we give you thanks, blessing, and praise.
Behold creation, so filled with miracles,
Benedictus es, benedictus es, Domine.

The gift of each day has been freely granted:
the gift of creation in glory revealed.
We thank you, Lord, for all its blessings,
we thank you, Lord, for the gift of each day,
your good gift of each day,
we thank you, Lord, for the gift of each day.
(John Rutter)

6. Believe in life
Believe in life as a stream ever flowing;
Believe in life as a tree ever growing:
The tree of life, with its branches high in the sky
and its roots so deep in the earth.

Believe in hope as a flame ever burning;
Believe in hope, like the springtime returning;
Believe in hope, lift your eyes up unto the hills,
whence comes our help from the Lord,
the Lord who made the heaven and earth.

Every step that you take could start a journey,
All the strangers you meet could turn to friends.
If you open your eyes new worlds will arise
if you just believe in your life,
believe in your hopes, believe in your dreams.

The stream rolls onward; all things must pass.
Our earthly days are short, all flesh as grass,
But through all ages long since time began,
There stands the tree of life, God's sign to man.
(John Rutter)

The tree of life my soul hath seen,
Laden with fruit, and always green;
The trees of nature fruitless be
Compared with Christ the apple tree. Amen.
(from the collection of Joshua Smith,
New Hampshire, 1784)